Book of Mormon 1-2-3s

Written by Kristena Eden

Illustrated by Linda Silvestri

To Kent, for his many years of love and support.
—Kristena

To my aunt Kay, who taught me,
"Life is uncertain—eat dessert first."
—Linda

ISBN 13: 978-1-4621-1651-5

Published by CFI, an imprint of Cedar Fort, Inc.
2373 W. 700 S., Springville, UT 84663
Distributed by Cedar Fort, Inc., www.cedarfort.com

Library of Congress Control Number: 2015954719

Cover design and typesetting by Shawnda T. Craig
Cover design © 2016 Cedar Fort, Inc.
Edited by Kevin Haws

Printed in the United States of America

10 9 8 7 6 5 4 3 2 1

Printed on acid-free paper

Lehi dreamed a dream.

In his dream, he saw **1 tree**

The tree represents Heavenly Father's love for us, and the fruit of the tree is there to make us happy.

1 Nephi 8

God commanded the families of Lehi and Ishmael to cross the sea.

1 Nephi 18:6, 8–9, and 23

These **2 families** went to the promised land in their ship. When they arrived in the promised land, they were happy and thanked Heavenly Father for their blessings.

Alma and Amulek were in a prison for 3 days, without food or water.

They prayed to Heavenly Father.

He kept them safe and helped them get free.

Alma 14:17–28

The 4 sons of Mosiah

wanted to go to the Lamanites as missionaries to teach about Jesus. They hoped that by sharing their love for Jesus the Lamanites would also learn to love Jesus.

Mosiah 28:1–9

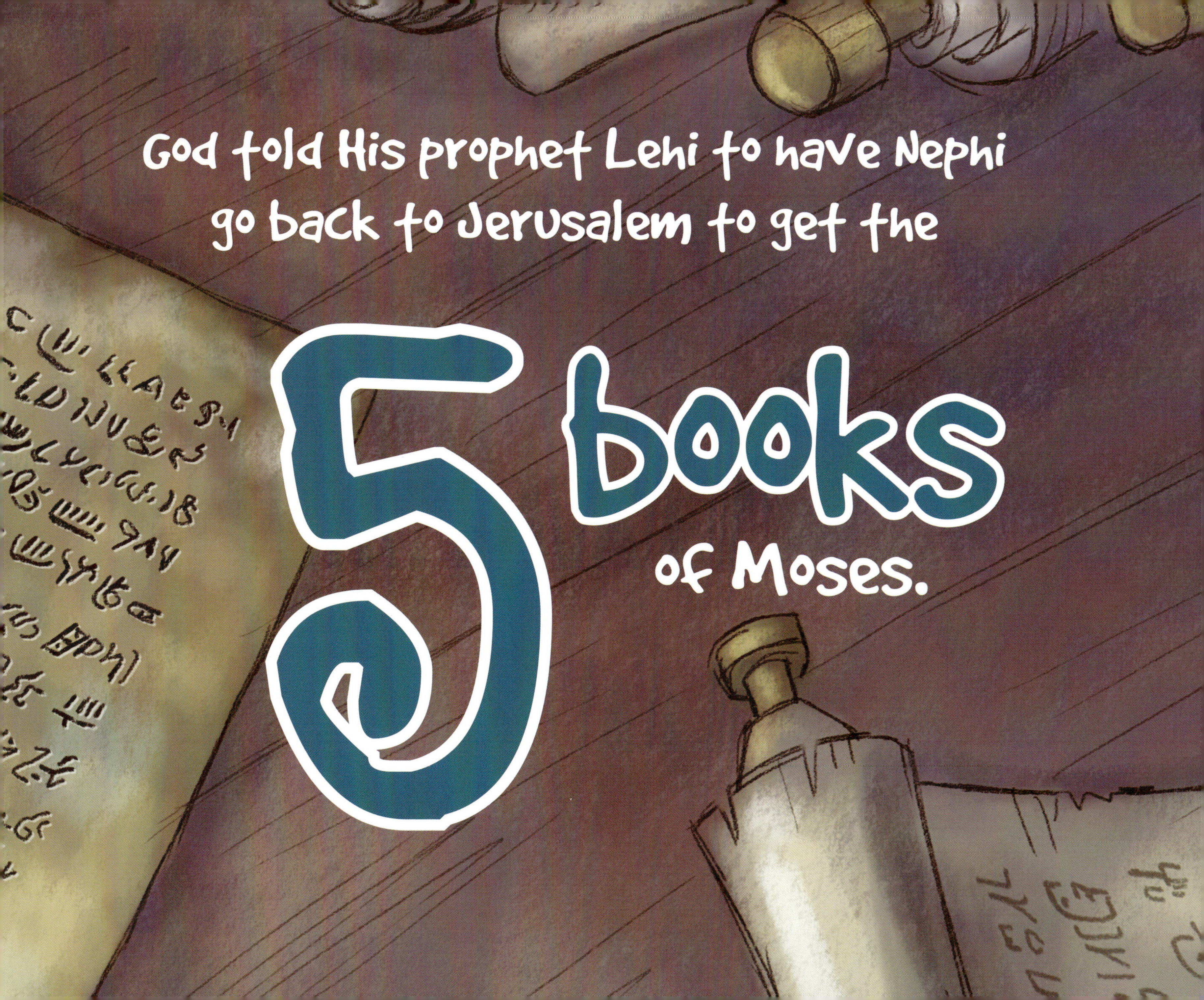

God told His prophet Lehi to have Nephi go back to Jerusalem to get the

5 books

of Moses.

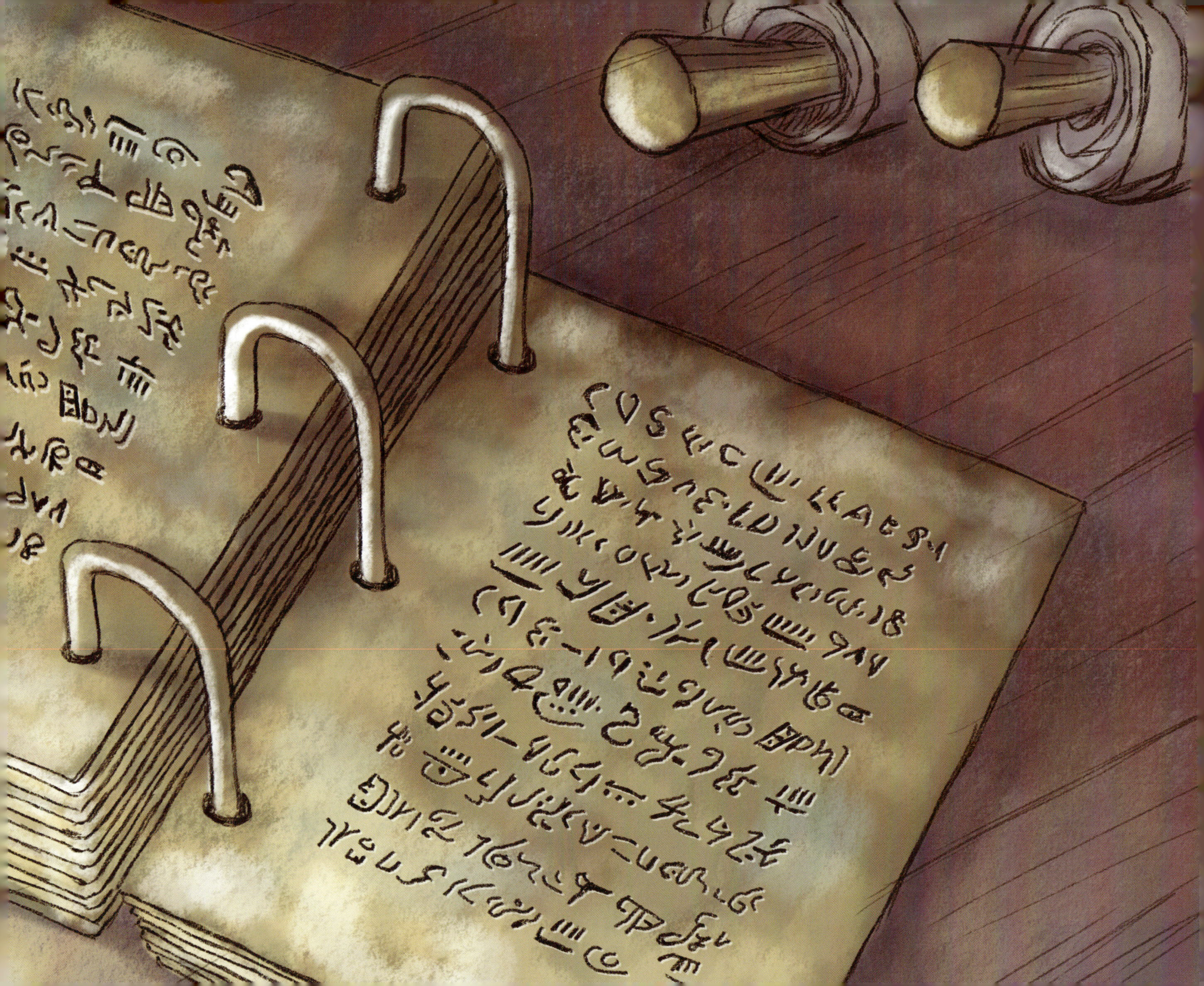

The 5 books of Moses tell us about Adam and Eve and the creation of the earth. Because Nephi followed God's commandment,

we are blessed to be able to read the scriptures.

1 Nephi 5:11

1 tree

2 families

3 days

4 sons

5 books

In Memor
our
Our Religion
Our Freedom
Our Peace
Our Wives
Our Children

Captain Moroni wanted his people to protect their freedom. He made a flag from his coat and called it

the title of liberty.

Alma 46:12–13

He wrote on it **6 things** to remember:

1- our God

2- our religion

3- our freedom

4- our peace

5- our wives

6- our Children

The Nephites were able to live on their food storage for

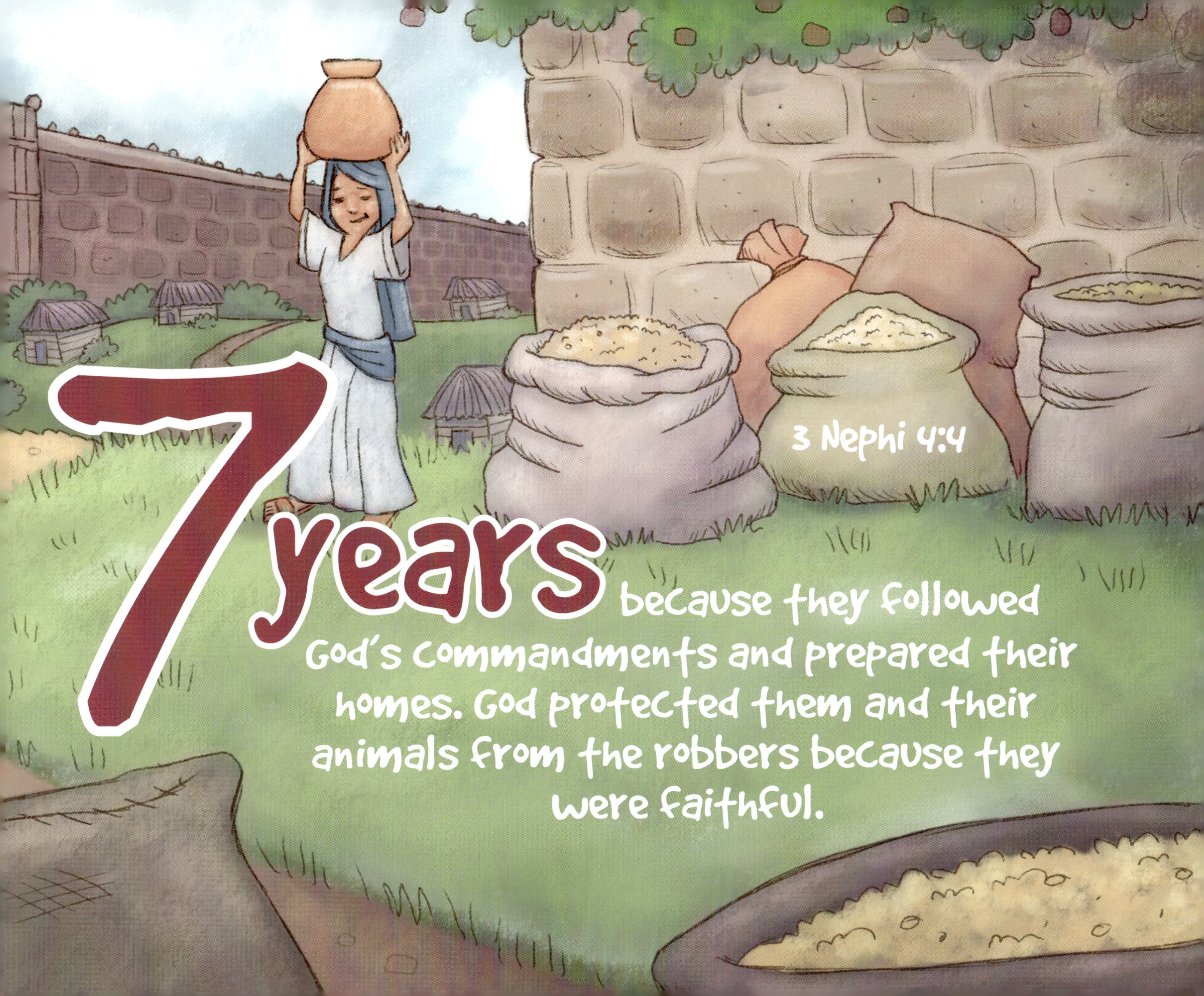

7 years

because they followed God's commandments and prepared their homes. God protected them and their animals from the robbers because they were faithful.

The brother of Jared was given instructions on how to build

Ether 2:16–25; 3:1–6

8 barges,

but he needed to find a way to light them. The brother of Jared made some special stones and asked Jesus to make the stones shine so the Jaredites would have light in the barges while they crossed the sea.

Jesus promised

9 disciples

that after they finished their mission on earth, they would go back to live with Heavenly Father. The other disciples wanted to stay on the earth and do missionary work until Jesus comes again.

3 Nephi 28:1–9

Jesus taught the Nephites about tithing.

Tithing is to pay one penny out of **10** or **10 cents** out of one dollar.

We pay tithing from the money we earn when we work.

Heavenly Father blesses us when we pay our tithing.

3 Nephi 24:8–10

1 tree 2 families 3 days

4 sons 5 books

6 things

7 years

8 barges

9 disciples

10 cents

The Author

Kristena Eden was born in oceanside, California, but she grew up around the world because her dad worked for the military. She has a degree in child development and was the owner and operator of Discovery Preschool. She also taught private kindergarten.

Kristena is the mother of six kids and the grandmother of nine. She currently lives with her husband and two dogs in Bluffdale, Utah, where she spends time developing her artistic talents with painting and pottery. Visit Kristena at www.kristenasfineart.com.

The Illustrator

Linda Silvestri is an illustrator who lives in Southern California, in a wee ranch-style house that she shares with Ignatz, a cranky calico, and her lovely husband, Tom. Her illustrations use a dash of traditional line work with generous doses of digital painting, peppered with plenty of whimsy. Linda loves her job and plays well with others. See more from Linda at www.lindasilvestri.com.

0 26575 16515 9